D1572449

SPEAKING
TO
WHAT
MATTERS

My story of learning how to share what's inside

KATHERINE KENNEDY

For Charlie, Joey and Kate

TABLE OF CONTENTS

PROLOGUE

I was sitting on my daughter's bed when she handed me a personal narrative she'd written for an eighth grade project. My eyes focused on the words *"She's not as confident as she seems but she has a big heart. A heart that she followed to start her own business helping people tell their story."* Oh my God she's talking about me. I was about to lock on to the sentence *"She's not as confident as she seems"* but my eyes skittered down the page to *"What I admire most about my mother is that she can laugh at herself."* Oh, thank God, at least she's learned *one thing* from me.

When I sat down to write this story, I wanted to create something that would be both honest and real, as well as helpful. I've read storytelling books that give frameworks, but are dry and boring. I've read memoirs of famous people where I still ache for more insight. So I didn't want to do that. Or that. I've also listened to thousands of stories about much more hardship than I've experienced. So, I couldn't do that. What I could do is offer *one thing*, my story, to show you a way to get closer to your own. And remind you that no matter how big or small your story may be, it matters.

As a storytelling coach, I've learned that to be able to tell your story, you need to get clear on the **challenges** you've faced, the **choices** you've made and the **change** that has revealed itself because of those choices. Yet the single most important thing I've learned about storytelling in this process is that our lives reveal the deepest message that we have to share with the world. In my story lives a journey of learning how to talk about what I felt deep inside and, in the process, get closer to myself and eventually to the people I care most about.

Laughing at myself is a skill I'm going to need. As the youngest in my family growing up, I can already hear the jokes coming down the pike about the writing of this book. *A story about yourself? It always was, Katherine!*

Yet this project has haunted me, and the events of 2020 almost made the telling of my story inevitable. When lockdowns from COVID hit, my husband was finishing a year of stage III colorectal cancer treatment and my father was dying. I gave myself the time, investment, and opportunity to make sense of my larger-than-life father, who was both the source of my core wound and the agent of my healing. My story—and the act of finding, writing, and telling the story—helped me crystallize the depth of the relationship we created over time. It's no wonder this story starts and ends with him.

That's what story work is. It's a way in. When you dig deep and look inside, you get more connected to who you are and the people who matter. You get to know, accept, and love yourself—the messy, imperfect parts you've kept hidden from others and possibly even yourself.

And it's a way out. You get to reframe your life's experiences and make whatever meaning you choose.

After you read this little book—or better yet, as you read—I hope you're inspired to tell your story and to discover the message your life is teaching you so that you can make an even bigger impact in the world. At the end of this story, I'll share more about a guide I've created to support you with this.

My path to creating intimate relationships based on honesty and love is rooted in these pages. So I invite you to come, get closer, and together we'll take a deeper look.

There's something we can learn from the stories we tell, and from every single story we hear.

Katherine

CHALLENGE

CHAPTER ONE

"It's nice to know we come from good people." – Dad

My dad carried stories of his childhood in his front pocket, like a well-used handkerchief. Never washed or upgraded. Right there, at his fingertips, carrying more and more importance over the years. And yet, whenever he told a story, his voice sounded like he was telling it for the very first time.

One of his favorites was about his and my mom's earliest fight. They were newlyweds and had just moved into a dark red brick row house on Ridgeville Street in Pittsburgh. He wasn't sure what he did wrong, but by the way she was stomping around, he *knew* he was in the wrong. She was mad. What it was about no one can recall.

"Do you still love me?" he asked her.

"Love has nothing to do with it," my mother retorted.

Growing up, I never had the heart to tell him I didn't understand what this one was all about.

I'm grateful I do now.

My dad was from the Irish Catholic side of town. Born a decade after the Depression, he developed his entrepreneurial skills selling the skins of muskrats and profiting from lost golf balls on a local public course in Rochester, New York where he grew up. His father was a builder who didn't graduate from college but worked hard to ensure his four children would.

When my dad was 12 years old, his oldest sibling Marty went into cardiac arrest after a routine operation on his thyroid and died. The surgeon happened to be their uncle. The death shook the entire family but, that day, my dad lost the most important person in his life.

After the funeral, his parents went into their bedroom, knelt at the bed, and recited the rosary. No tears, no wails of injustice. Just the quiet murmur of praying.

As a little girl, when I heard this story, this was one lesson I understood clearly. Put your fate and faith in God and when your prized first son or beloved older brother dies *don't feel sorry for yourself.*

While my dad was the kind of kid who was taught to do the right thing, he admits after the death of his older brother, he sometimes couldn't help himself. He was hurting and acted out much to the dismay of the nuns.

One time, shortly after Marty died, my dad played a joke on Bobby Cucinelli on the playground. "Why can't you be more like your older brother?" Sister Mary Paul uttered as she sent him off to detention. His punishment was to stand at the chalkboard and write *"I am a bad boy, I am a bad boy, I am a bad boy"* over and over again. Knowing his profound loss, how could a nun mutter those words to a little boy who just lost his brother? Why did she have him write *those* words? It still makes me shudder when I think about it.

That day a persistent tremor started in my father's right hand. I think that's what must happen to pain. It's in there. Even if it doesn't know how to come out, it always finds a way.

Like my dad, my mother was raised Catholic in Rochester, New York and was the youngest in her family, too. My mom's family owned a tissue paper mill, the kind you find in a light blue Tiffany box. She attended an all-women's Catholic college in Washington DC that expected their students to *'always look their best'* and had a short career as a runway model for department stores. As a little girl, I marveled that my own mother made it into a *Mademoiselle* college edition highlighting put-together young women on campus. With her long legs and hazel eyes, she was a beauty.

My mom grew up with a mother who'd announce, "I'm going on strike," as she shut the door to her bedroom...for days. It took until my adulthood to understand that Grandma married a nice man, but Grandpa was not the man she loved. My mom felt loved by her parents but understood their marriage had everything to do with love for their children but not for each other.

My parents met on a blind date in high school but didn't date for very long. After they graduated from college, they got back together, and my dad asked her to marry him. Knowing she had reservations about marriage from her mother's experience, he added, "I can make you happy." And with that, my 23-year-old mom answered, "Yes."

****

In 1962, after six months serving in the Army Reserve, my dad moved with my mom to Pittsburgh. He had a job as a loan officer at Mellon Bank, but dreamed of being an entrepreneur. He loved telling the story of his grandfather Alfred J. Mansmann who left school in the 2nd grade to work in a glass factory, and at the age of 25, opened a successful department store. It was a lifelong dream to follow in those footsteps and be his own boss.

But he had to figure out how to get capital because he didn't have any money. So after seven years as a loan officer, he borrowed money from his parents, his in-laws and the bank to purchase a fledgling secretarial business.

For most of my grade school years, my father's ambition came with a lot of hard work and time away from the family. He traveled all over the country to the different secretarial schools during the week and spent time on the golf course making deals and cementing friendships on the weekends. Yet his success catapulted our family into a suburb called Fox Chapel with rolling hills, tree-lined streets and beautiful homes…and the assumption that our lives were perfect.

My dad's ambition was matched by his warmth and optimism. He was the kind of guy who would light up a room with his magnetic personality and big smile.

My dad often marveled that his grandfather Calihan, who was in politics, had the largest funeral ever to be held in the city of Rochester. Of course this was back in 1899 but being a politician carried a certain reverence that my dad admired and maybe secretly wished upon himself. I think he loved how my mom would often refer to him as *'The Mayor.'*

I remember how he'd look right in people's eyes, put out his hand, and give the kind of handshake that stated, *'I'm genuinely happy to see you.'* I can still hear how he'd say his name *'Joe Calihan'* with a slightly baritone voice and a sprinkle of charm. When he'd come home from work, walk through the back door into the kitchen, we'd ask him how he was and he'd say, *"Better now!"*

As a little girl, I wanted to be just like him and make people feel the way he did. He was my role model.

I have fond memories of Saturday night mass at the Sacred Heart Church—although that wasn't really the "fond" part of the memory:). After mass, all six of us would pile into our navy-blue Buick station wagon and pull up and buy the next day's paper from a shaky old man on Negley Avenue. We'd charge in the house to eat Fritos with Kroger's French onion dip in the living room and flank steak that had been marinated all day in Wishbone Italian. We'd eat dinner in the dining room and play Michigan Poker as my dad sat at the head of the table like the CEO he was.

And yet, I grew up in the hands-*off* parenting movement of the

70's and 80's. In those early years, most of the day-to-day parenting was left to my mom. Preoccupied, my mother was busy with housework, making dinner, driving four kids around, sewing, cleaning, the list goes on and on. I got the sense she was sacrificing herself and I wanted to make her happy if I could, too.

I was the 4th child, the baby. I felt loved, but the juice box was empty. I misinterpreted my mother's busyness for distance. Or maybe her distance for busyness. All I knew was, there were so many needs around and mine were at the bottom of the totem pole.

My older sister Molly and I – we were known as *'The Girls.'* We shared a bedroom with Raggedy Ann and Andy bedspreads and red and white checkered drapes. We all had our roles. Molly was the nice one. My older brother Marty, named after my father's late brother, was the smart one. My oldest sister, Anne, she was the pretty one.

What set me apart from my siblings is that I could make everyone laugh. Once I caught wind of a saying, a gesture, a moment, I would not let it go. After spotting a picture of Jacqueline Onassis Kennedy on the White House tour in Washington DC, I couldn't help myself. I loved the way Jac-leen rolled off my tongue: *"Jacleen Jacleen Jacleen."* When we went to New York City to see our first Broadway show, *Sophisticated Ladies,* I crowed: *"Doo Wap Doo Wap Doo Wap,"* for the 7-hour ride home. In those moments my mom would say, "Oh Katherine, you're too much," but she would laugh too. I might not have been very sophisticated, but they thought I was funny and let's face it, I found my role in the family. I was the *fun* one.

Long before the influences of social media came along, how we looked on the outside seemed to matter more than how we felt on the inside. *"Are you good?"* My young brain told me the answer always needed to be *'yes.'* With my Dorothy Hammill haircut, my pot belly and larger frame, the amount of time I focused on how bad I looked was immeasurable and downright unfortunate. Being stuck and focused on what you are *not* takes a lot of energy from what you *are.*

Years of Catholic School recitations: *"Lord I am not worthy to receive you but only say the word and I shall be healed,"* meant that, at school, I wasn't good enough either. Sister Alicia, the Principal, confirmed this with her stares of steel rage and disgust. I can still remember how my butt would shake when I saw her grimace. I didn't know the word *glute* back then but I'm pretty sure that was the muscle group directly connected to my fear. My mind would freeze and go blank when I saw her in the hallway. I always felt like I was in trouble. She scared me to death.

My parents used the same *"don't-feel-sorry-for-yourself"* messages they grew up with. I internalized this to mean don't feel bad…Well, about anything. Our lives were on the up and up. We were *'The Calihans.'* We were cool, fun, and hard-working. We were also Catholics in a sea of what we called "WASPs" [white anglo saxon protestants]. Yes, we had a little chip on our shoulders, but that made us feel proud. And what on earth did we have to feel bad about anyway?

As I took the yellow school bus over the hill to the little working class Catholic school I attended for eight years, I might have felt bad about a lot of things. Yet I also knew being the daughter of Joe and Brenda Calihan meant being from the other side of the tracks, the lucky side.

CHAPTER TWO

"Fake it til you make it." - Dad

When I was thirteen, I was walking down the front stairs one night when I noticed someone was in the study. It was late and dark, and I heard a hushed voice. I tiptoed as I reached the last green carpeted stair, peeked through the narrow crack in the wood paneled door and saw my dad sitting at the mahogany desk with a single desk light on. The way he was sitting still in the stillness of the night felt strange to me, so I crouched down to huddle in the hallway behind the door.

He was on the phone with someone. It wasn't my mother because my mom, well, she was upstairs. I heard my dad talking in a voice he usually reserved for my mom. I heard him say, "You're my alter ego." I didn't know what that meant but it felt like my dad shouldn't be talking to another woman that way. My heart stopped. I felt something in my chest welling up and didn't know what to do with it.

I was in my ruffled Lanz pajamas as I ran out of the front door and tried to get the tone of his voice out of my head. As I paced in the yard, I felt something inside me crumble along with the ideal of what our family was all about. That's when I opened my mouth and screamed. Silently, of course. I didn't want to upset the neighbors or let my dad know that I'd heard him.

I was only in 8th grade, but this night confirmed something I had been feeling for a long time. *It was all too good to be true.* The night I spied on my dad, I resigned myself to the fact that maybe we were no different at all. Not better. Not worse. Not lucky. Not charmed. And there was no one I could talk to about it.

****

That summer, after graduating from 8th grade, I ended up at the hospital with a gash on my leg and Old Grand Dad bourbon flooding my whole body. This was the second time I ended up in the ER because of drinking too much and I was barely 13. I was heading into high school and was hanging out with all the private school kids. In a drunken stupor one night, I jumped the fence in our backyard and wound up with a 3-inch cut on the inside of my thigh that needed 17 stitches. My mom and dad were at a cocktail party, so my siblings took me to the hospital.

I still to this day don't know why I drank myself into oblivion at such a young age. I do remember when that liquor hit my system thinking, *Oh this is nice. I don't have to feel what I usually feel.* It was like discovering an escape hatch. One that I would continue to have to reckon with.

I was supposed to be on my way to summer camp, but my parents had no choice but to delay my trip for a day. When I got home from the hospital, they sat me down in the kitchen and probed, "Katherine, we love you. We need to ask you why this happened."

I didn't have the words to explain it. I didn't have the where-with-al or the courage to try and express what I was feeling. We were surrounded by so much, but all I could see was what I wasn't. I wasn't beautiful like my oldest sister, smart like my brother or as nice as Molly. I knew there were kinks in my parents' armor but didn't want to say anything. The private school kids intimidated me and I had not a single athletic bone in my body. I was stuck in *'the wasn'ts'* but surrounded by so much, I didn't dare complain. I didn't want to let my parents in on how I was feeling: *sorry for myself.* That would have been like a cardinal sin.

If I could talk myself out of feeling what I was feeling...then everything might be okay. *Don't rock the boat, put a smile on your face, keep everything status quo,* I said to myself. It was worth a try.

I wanted my parents to ask me some more questions. But they just looked at me. Didn't say a word. Nor did I. I was just looking at the floorboards, asking, in my own way, that same old question my dad had asked my mom: *Do-you-still-love-me?* I wish I had known then that their silence didn't mean they didn't love me. Maybe they just didn't know what to say.

****

By the time I went to high school, I was living between two extremes: On the outside I looked like I had my shit together, a hard-working student, boyfriends, lots of friends, the life of the party. Senior year, I was Student Council President. Endlessly trying to live up to the image of being a Calihan and fit into the right box.

On the inside, the silence in me started to fester, creating a deep abyss of resentment and self-loathing. I wasn't sure who was betraying who. The actions of my dad or the silence of myself.

It was all so very confusing. My parents traveled together, they drank a 6pm scotch together and appeared to be the perfect couple. I was the last one at home. My siblings were off in college. I didn't know what was normal, but the tension I could feel between them didn't match up to the image they conveyed. I wish I could have told my younger self that marriage can be like that— you can love them and want to stick a fork in them—but I didn't know if this was garden-variety problems or something seismic.

And something else felt off. We were chasing the American dream; there were new cars, a remodeled kitchen and ski vacations. The more we started to have, the less safe things started to feel. I wondered, *Was money on our side? Was it something to celebrate or disdain?*

I couldn't put my finger on what was going on, but it seemed to me the elusive dream of having *more* was creating an inverse relationship with our happiness. What was the point of all this abundance if no one was talking to each other??? What mattered to me was how I felt on the inside but speaking about it didn't seem like an option.

I took my cues and kept my mouth shut.

****

When I was a senior in high school and 17 years old, I did a stupid thing. I'm sure most of us can recall at least one stupid thing we did when we were 17 but this one upset the apple cart. I'd fallen head over heels for a fellow counselor at an overnight camp where I worked that summer in South Carolina. Greg had a southern accent, played the guitar, and made me feel loved. We spent our time off hiking in the Blue Mountains, drinking White Zinfandel and having sex in the back of his light sky-blue Jeep Laredo. His desire for me filled me up, and I couldn't get enough.

That fall as a senior in high school, I asked my parents if he could join us skiing over Christmas break and they readily agreed. When I went to wake him up in his room the last morning of our trip, he pulled me lovingly into bed with him. I whispered to myself, *I shouldn't do this,* but brushed those thoughts aside as I took off my nightgown and got on top of him.

It was at that exact moment my father had come up to the loft to wake us up. I heard something by the door and saw plaid pajamas flutter by. Fear jolted through my body as I jumped off Greg, got out of bed and put my clothes on. I ran into the hallway, and standing at the railing from the loft above, I locked eyes with my dad.

You have to understand my father was raised believing sex before marriage was wrong, wrong, wrong. I had done *the unspeakable.* Tears were rolling down his cheeks as he looked up at me and remonstrated, "How could you do that?"

We all sat in silence in the van to the airport. *What an idiot. You're the worst. What an asshole.* No one had to say that to me because I was saying that all to myself.

When we got home, my mother tried to console me with a pat on the back of my hand. She didn't agree with how my father was reacting, but she wasn't too pleased with her daughter either. I knew her very *Catholic* Catholic upbringing made it hard for her to accept what I had done, too. Pre-marital sex was wrong in her eyes, too, and I was only 17, to boot.

What I didn't know was that one day of my father not talking to me would turn into months of him not acknowledging my presence. When he came home from the office, there was no *"Better now!"* When we were at the dinner table, nothing was spoken. He wouldn't let his eyes land on mine. I felt like he was trying to erase me from his existence. I was shut out and the pain of that isolation was almost unbearable.

My dad's response confirmed my deepest fear: *If I was who I really am, I wouldn't be loved.*

Back then, I had never even heard of the word shame. But this was shame of the worst kind. The kind that shames itself.

*****

A couple months later, I was rushing to class after leading an all-school Monday meeting when the school counselor saw me and said, "Hey Katherine, come in my office for a minute, I want to talk to you about something."

Tom Johnson was a broad chested Black man who wore a clerical collar and walked around campus with a smile and kind demeanor that conveyed *I care about you.* I didn't understand how he was a Reverend *and* a high school counselor but never took the time to ask. When he asked me to pop into his light-filled office, I followed him and sat down in the chair across from him.

"I see you working so hard on behalf of everyone. I can often hear your laugh in the hallway. But sometimes I look at you and wonder if you are okay." He paused, then added, "Are you okay?"

It was as if Sister Alicia, my catholic school Principal, had been reincarnated because despite his calm and soothing voice, the pit of my stomach clenched, and my chest tightened. *Was I in trouble?* The nerve endings of every part of my body were on high alert. I thought I had become adept at hiding what I was feeling. *How did he know? Who else could tell?*

The room had three glass walls allowing the kids walking by to see in. I felt as exposed as my orange goldfish Speedy. *Play it cool, Katherine. Everyone can see you,* I said to myself.

I didn't say a word out loud, I couldn't speak. But tears rolled down my cheeks and didn't stop. Dear Reverend Johnson didn't ask me to tell him what those tears were about, but his deep brown eyes sat with me in the silence of my pain.

If those tears could have talked, they would have said, "I'm alone, I'm miserable, and I'm _so_ tired of pretending everything is okay."

CHAPTER THREE

"Use good judgment." - Dad

The whites of my eyes were as dry as the top of my tongue. I could still taste the Jack and Coke and grinned as I recalled my favorite Talking Heads line *My God what have I done?* My vision came into focus as I felt the sweetness of relief. *Phew.* I was still dressed in the forest green turtleneck and black wool pants (with a thick nylon liner) outfit I was wearing the night before. It was the early 90's. I was a freshman in college. *At least I wasn't wearing shoulder pads.* And given my track record, thank God, I was alone.

Littered on my sweater were little bits of hairballs from a cat I must have cuddled somewhere along the night. I'm allergic to cats. More troubling was the dried ketchup, specks of vinegar and processed cheese that was stuck to the wool, reminding me about the late night food fest at Billibob's, a local diner famous for late night cheesesteaks and french fries.

At that moment, in the expanse of the white sheets and me, I had an epiphany. I *knew* what I was going to give up for my new year's resolution come January 1st. I *knew* what I needed to do to feel more in control. Wait for it. Wait for it. I was going to give up *french fries!*

I was smug with pride. No more would I have food smothered

on my clothes. No more would I be horrified by how much I ate the night before. Happy with myself and my new declaration, I leaned over, fished out the pack of *Marlboro Lights* from my black velvet purse on the hardwood floor, and lit a cigarette.

I had gotten into Penn, an Ivy League school, and more importantly, my father's alma mater. Growing up, my father would always say, "Use good judgment." I managed to tune that out, *but I still heard it*. As I left for college, my mother feebly offered one piece of advice, "Be the person you want to be, Katherine." I agreed with my parents, yet I was digging myself further into what felt like an abyss.

I was chain smoking. Not just cigarettes but boyfriends, too. Starting a new relationship before I had extinguished the one I was with. *"Next!"* my parents would exclaim with a laugh and a trace of embarrassment.

I called it all fun, but was it?

No amount of booze could numb my feelings, yet alcohol played a role. The late nights, the black outs, and the hookups were as easy as flicking on a light switch and kept me using the best trick in my toolbox: *distraction*.

Using a cocktail of shame and denial, I kept making myself the problem.

Like the night I sprained my ankle as I raced down the stairs of an off-campus fraternity house to get away from the boy who just penetrated me. I was too far gone to get myself out of what could be best described as a precarious situation. I didn't call it rape then. In my 18-year-old mind, it was just a drunken escapade that I had brought on myself. I *deserved* to be on crutches. I was the fool.

****

The summer after freshman year, I went on a community service program to Kenya with my sister Molly for two months. Every morning we would walk three miles to teach math at the village school. Late afternoons were spent cooking, cleaning and laughing with our host family. At night we would crawl into sleeping bags covered with mosquito netting and reflect on the day and our lives back home. Day by day, week by week, we started to talk about our feelings with a level of depth that felt new to me.

It may sound cliche but the chance to step out of my comfort zone helped me see the loving, generous, centered person I could be. I returned full of optimism and determined to start taking myself more seriously, to engage in deeper, more authentic conversations like I had with Molly, to let people see more of the *real* Katherine.

Yet, when I returned to school that fall, the lessons I learned about myself soon faded from my awareness. I would go to off campus parties and shake with fear as I guzzled flat, warm beer down my throat, wishing I could tell them about the depth of my experience on a different continent. I was sure no one would really care. People saw the same life of the party Katherine. Eventually, I threw in the towel and went back to the same old ways. The distractions of college life, the expectation to be the same, the addiction to feeling bad came roaring back. I certainly wasn't listening to my father's advice of using good judgment or my mother's advice of being the person I wanted to be. It was almost like I knew no other way.

I survived my junior year in one piece but, after a one-night stand the last semester of college, I peed on a stick a week later and saw two lines; I stopped breathing. It wasn't the first time I bought a pregnancy kit, but it was the first time it was positive. I wasn't upset with anyone except myself. I had a whiff of thinking, *Of course you couldn't make it through college without this happening. Bad bad bad. You deserve this,* I told myself. My negative thinking spun in circles unchecked.

I reached out to my African Art History professor and met her outside of the Fisher Library. She was petite with short brown hair that feathered to the side. Sitting on the cement ledge in front of the library, I asked to drop the class.

She offered, "I'd be happy to help you," and then she paused. She looked right at me and asserted, "I'm here if you want to talk about what's going on."

I felt the grip in my throat. I wanted to tell her. Everything. I was desperate for her to not let me off the hook.

Instead, almost automatically, I looked back at her and replied, "No, I can still graduate on time without this class. I'm good." I thanked her, jumped up and scurried up the sidewalk.

The next day Molly took a day off work and drove up from Washington DC to take me to the abortion clinic. She sat with me as I cried in the recovery room.

"You're going to be okay, Kath," she assured me.

We knew that this was the right choice, but we also knew this was something to keep from Mom and Dad.

CHOICE

CHAPTER FOUR

"With privilege goes responsibility." - Dad

I noticed her hair first. Brown and long, with a seventies style reserved for beautiful women. She looked to me like a *Charlie's Angel.*

"You can call me Linda," she said with a hint of a midwestern drawl.

Linda and my parents met at a conference, and she came to stay with us one night. At the time I was in high school and had never met a real live therapist. She didn't chit chat much and that was unusual in our family. I wondered if it was because of her profession or that she was from a place in Northern California called Bolinas where all the hippies lived.

She talked about a nonprofit she was starting called *Summer Search* which was helping kids go on wilderness programs and be the first in their families to go to college. I was intrigued. My mom had been a teacher early on and my dad was the CEO of the secretarial business. Naturally, I thought I would be a teacher or the head of an organization. Linda offered a fresh perspective on other ways I could help people.

Three months later, as a thanks for a donation my dad made,

we got a letter from one of the students in her program. The story painted a picture of the student's life and towards the end included very clear insight about what he learned on his summer program. It was all so very honest. I was standing at the kitchen island and felt my heart explode.

For years, Linda kept popping into my head.

She was the person I called when I wanted to do something meaningful during a summer in college. She was the one who suggested that community service program in Kenya.

Linda was the person I called senior year of college when I got into Teach For America. I reached out to her because I actually wanted her to hire me, but instead she brushed me off when she suggested, "Why don't you get some real experience and call me in two years?"

She was the person I called as soon as I finished my first year of teaching. Again, I told her I still hoped to work with her. This was the time she finally asked me to come visit her during the student interview season.

"You'll understand how I work with the students, and it will either appeal to you, or not," she stated matter of factly.

****

I flew to San Francisco to stay with a college roommate near Ghirardelli Square. Linda picked me up in her brown Lexus sedan that smelled of worn leather. We headed over the Bay Bridge as the sun rose, and I could feel the promise of a new start. As we approached Oakland High, hundreds of high school students were walking through the parking lot. Linda pulled into a spot that had a faded-out *Faculty* painted on the asphalt.

Georganne Ferrier, the teacher who nominated the students we would be working with, was standing by the double doors greeting everyone. When she saw us, she gasped with delight. Her key chain jangled with every step as she led us into the one-story building through the cafeteria and down a long hallway with royal blue lockers to a door and then stopped. I was almost expecting to see a mop and a bucket when she unlocked the door but instead there were three chairs and a desk. The room was small and windowless.

"Oh, Georganne this is perfect," Linda said to my surprise.

Linda immediately put her hand in her giant brown leather purse and whipped out a Kleenex box acknowledging that "sometimes the interviews get a little emotional." She placed a Polaroid camera next to a pen and yellow pad of legal sized paper.

Georganne continued to talk as Linda set up the chairs. I was starting to wonder if some of the students of color in the school would be bothered by three white women trying to be do-gooders. Linda interrupted my spinning thoughts and whispered to me, "Always put the student's chair at an angle from you," adding, "The interviews are personal, and this gives them a little psychological space."

Before we knew it, there was a student hovering by the door in the busy hallway. Georganne saw her and exclaimed, "Oh you are just going to love Chai!"

Linda gave Chai a handshake and asked her to sit in the metal chair at the end of the desk. She pointed with a blank face to my chair and asked the student permission that I sit in on her interview. Chai nodded. I noticed Linda wasn't chit chatting. I knew my job was to stay still and silent, and in that moment, I was relieved. I wouldn't have known what to say anyway.

We sat in our assigned chairs as I witnessed the interview unfold.

There was no small talk or lengthy introductions, just one simple line.

Linda pointed to Chai's shoes under the table and said, "See your shoes? The goal of this interview is for me to get inside *those* shoes."

The words hit me in the gut like a ton of bricks.

Linda didn't move a muscle. I tracked Chai's eyes as she also processed the question; they froze. I knew at that moment she understood the depth of this question and the courage it was going to take to answer it.

A few seconds later, almost suddenly, the energy shifted. It was like the molecules in the room were pulling us closer. The student looked at Linda. Linda's piercing green eyes looked right back, and, with a whisper, the student began describing her journey to America.

"I'm Chinese but was born in a refugee camp in Vietnam. I took a boat to the Philippines when I was 10, lived there for four years and last year, my mother and I came here. We live in a one room studio in Chinatown."

Linda's eyes were glued on Chai. "Sounds like you have been through a lot. What's been the hardest part?"

"Living in refugee camps was hard and waiting, not knowing how long we would be anywhere." The young woman paused and looked straight into the empty space Linda had created by putting the chairs at an angle. She continued, "But the hardest part for me has been coming here and never seeing my mom. She works as a housekeeper in a hotel downtown and at night she works in a sewing factory."

As the student talked, teardrops formed in the far corners of her eyes. Seeing hers I tried to hold back my own.

****

Four more emotionally charged interviews went by just like that one. Linda pulled out a can of Coke from her purse and asked me if I wanted one. Realizing I was supposed to bring my lunch, I immediately accepted. We took a bathroom break and as we walked back, another student was standing in the hallway outside the interview room. The girl was African American, wore black rimmed glasses and gave me a firm handshake as she said, "Hi, I'm Angela."

Once we shuffled inside the broom-closet-like room, closed the heavy door, and sat down on our assigned chairs, Linda turned to me and asked if I wanted to start the interview. I felt a tidal wave of adrenaline and fear through the inside of my bones but responded with, "Yes, that would be great."

A few minutes later, I stumbled through the *what's-it-like-to-be-in-your-shoes* question and then waited. So did Angela. In fact, she just stared at me.

My heart was beating fast. I didn't know what to say. I wanted to look and sound competent and had a flashback of Linda probing about what they did during the summer. So I asked, "What did you do during your summers?"

She responded, "What do you want to know?"

A ping pong game of short questions and answers started and didn't end until Linda swooped in and saved us both. Linda led with a statement and asked a simple open-ended question, "You're carrying a lot of responsibilities Angela, I'd love to hear more." Linda's voice was firm yet soft. And then she waited.

Linda was doing something that I had never seen before. *She stopped talking.* I felt myself shift in my chair. The silence haunted me. But Linda was in charge of the conversation and had created a space that allowed this young woman to step into it.

Within a moment, Angela told her about taking care of her disabled mother and how hard she worked in school. Her voice cracked every time she mentioned her mother.

I was stunned. I saw why Linda was making such a big deal of these interviews. In less than an hour, a glue-like connection was being created by two people. I had never seen anything like it. Not in the world. Not in my family. I certainly didn't have any of this rare courage back when my high school counselor Tom Johnson pulled me into his office.

Something stirred. It felt like a craving. Maybe I could learn how to connect with people in this kind of way, too?

We drove back across the Richmond bridge to Linda's office in a bungalow in Mill Valley. She offered me a bottle of Moosehead beer which I gratefully accepted. It had been a long day.

After a swig, I couldn't play it cool. I *needed* to work with her. I blurted out, "Linda, I'd really like to work with you!" She winked at me. We clinked our beers, said, *"Cheers!"* and made a plan. I would finish out my two-year commitment to Teach For America and then would move out to the Bay Area to start working with Summer Search.

One thing was for certain: My life would never be the same.

****

I was Linda's first hire. And for the first three months, she sat in on every single one of my student interviews. *"Do this, don't do that, try it this way."* I like to think of those months of interviewing students for 10 hours a day like Navy Seal training, just in airless closets usually reserved for school supplies with a middle-aged woman as my fearless sergeant. Each day felt like climbing up on the high dive. I was eager to get wet, but afraid of heights.

I often didn't know what to say but learned that silence was a powerful mechanism to draw out the truth. Over time my ping pong matches shifted to longer, deeper conversations.

I was learning how to bring up hard subjects from losing a parent or struggling with depression. I was learning how to give students the space to open up. I was learning how to listen. But most of all, I was learning how to help students feel safe enough to be vulnerable, to share what was inside.

While Linda was watching me, I was watching students shift in their chairs after being listened to. I was floored by their honesty. I couldn't get enough. I learned not to focus on their circumstances, like the student who was living out of a car with her father, or the one who just opened up about his sexuality for the first time. I focused on their courage. I didn't feel pity. I felt awe. I had been trying to find a way to speak about the things that truly mattered my whole life but always kept a lid on it. I didn't have the words. I didn't have the confidence. I was too afraid.

In the span of an hour, I could feel their pain, hear their sorrows, and see them completely. They were brave enough, more than I was at their age, to let a stranger in their shoes.

In the process of learning how to help people tell their story, I realized I had something of value to offer: *myself.* I would do *anything* I could to help students find the words to express themselves. And if they could step up, well then maybe I could, too.

CHAPTER FIVE

"Act enthusiastic and you'll be enthusiastic." - Dad

During one particularly long day of interviews at Oakland High School, I snuck outside on top of the hot asphalt and under the California blue skies to have a cigarette. Back then, I smoked a pack a day. I had just asked a student to let me in their shoes and here I was crouching behind the auditorium inhaling on a white stick like my life depended on it. I tried to hide it from Linda just like I did with my parents. I was embarrassed as I knew what began as an act of rebellion in high school was now an addictive habit.

I had been learning from Linda how to help students look 'under the hood' and begin to examine why they did certain things, like forgetting to call, not turning forms in on time, or missing an important event. Behaviors that could derail their success. For me, smoking had been a way to rebel, to tune out and to feel bad. As I stood there sucking down my cigarette standing out on that black top, I found myself saying, *What does this say about you Katherine? How would you feel if one of your students saw you? Why are you so committed to feeling bad about yourself?* That was the kicker. The minute I saw, I mean really saw, how this habit was self-defeating and had the potential to sabotage any chance I was creating to feel good about myself, I knew what I needed to do. I needed to *walk the walk* as a mentor and interrupt my behavior.

There was something else that I was noticing about myself that was troubling. Every single time Linda would confront me about anything (even if it was just to ask where the paper was for the printer) I would freeze. And then go silent. I wanted to please her. Show her what a good girl I was. I felt caught every time she asked me about a task I hadn't completed.

I hadn't worked through conflict or difficult conversations. I had always run the other direction. Or, like when I was thirteen and just back from the hospital, I stayed silent and looked at the floorboards. The *'fake it til you make it'* part of me helped me be perceived as confident. Linda had even described me as *plucky*, but the veneer of confidence was starting to crumble.

Day after day, night after night, I found myself saying to my students, *"It takes courage to talk about the hard stuff,"* but I wasn't yet able to do the same. How could I truly be an effective mentor when I hadn't really demonstrated that kind of courage to myself?

A year into working with Linda, an opportunity presented itself to go on one of the very trips Summer Search would send students on. I jumped at the chance. It was called Outward Bound. I figured I would be able to better understand what happened on wilderness programs and also get a much-needed break.

I had started running after work every day as a way to let go of some of the heavy feelings I was absorbing as a mentor but was still deathly afraid of anything too physically-taxing or scary like rock-climbing. So I did the opposite of what I told my students to do and picked the easiest trip: canoeing and backpacking for nine days with adults up in the North Cascades of Washington. I had been a camp counselor in high school and taught canoeing. Much better than scaling the side of a mountain, right?

It was on Day 7 when my group was sitting around a campfire and a question emerged that I wasn't expecting. *'What in the wilderness most resembles you?'* I scanned the forest trying to find just the right thing. My eyes locked on the soft, green moss that was providing some warmth and cushion where I was sitting. I could feel a lump in my throat. I'm like that damn moss. Kind to others but hiding what was underneath: a deep dark mess. But wait. I didn't want to be the moss. The big open sky was above. I wanted to be that or a tree with deep roots and far-reaching branches or even a soaring eagle.

I hated moss. But I couldn't ignore the questions it evoked for me. *Why did I still feel so committed to trying to hide the mess underneath? What if I admitted I didn't have my shit together? What are you so afraid of, Katherine?* As the campfire crackled, I spilled all of this out to a group of strangers. They responded with loving eyes and head nodding. I didn't even need to tell them what all those dark feelings were to feel understood. One by one, we each opened up about all the things we hid from others.

The second to last day was "the solo," a whole 24 hours of being by yourself in the woods. The *Summer Search* students had told me stories of their solos which were basically 3 days of foraging for food and being alone amidst the elements of the outdoors. I thought one day of this by comparison would be simple.

I walked away from my group and turned into a stretch of the forest by myself. There was no designated path for me to take, only the instructions to walk for an hour before even making camp for the night. I walked until I found a clearing in the forest. The silence and solitude felt eerie to me. I sat down on a patch of dry leaves and felt a wave of emotion rip through my body.

I cried *for hours*. I cried for all things I kept inside, and I cried for all the ways I hated myself. And for the little girl who wasn't good enough, who hated her body, her face and felt all alone in the world. I cried for all the times I put other people's needs first. And for the ways I had either lied or hurt the people around me. I had never cried that way or for that long. Ever.

The trip, just like my life, was supposed to have been easy, but it sure didn't feel that way. The walls had come down in the North Cascades and when I returned to San Francisco my anxiety was at an all-time high. So many feelings had bubbled to the surface, and I didn't know what to do with them. I wanted to be more of the person I had experienced during my Outward Bound but didn't know how to get back to her.

I saw this play out with our students and had even experienced this when I went to Kenya that one summer: Explosive opportunities to grow in a short amount of time often lead one to return home to the same old environment and, without intention, go back to the same old self. I recognized I was on a similar journey just like my students. If I was going to truly transform what was possible for myself, I had to give myself permission to feel what I was feeling.

I knew I needed to talk to someone, but that scared me. Therapy to me was still some California version of confession. The thought of talking about my family's imperfections felt like I was choosing betrayal, as if I was stepping outside the family code.

But when I got back, I put those fears aside and found another middle-aged woman with a deep soothing radio voice. In our first session she said something I had never heard before. She insisted, "*Shame derives its power from being unspoken.*" Shame was the reason I bottled everything under that moss. Shame was the reason I didn't feel I could be myself. Shame, I soon found out, had been running the show.

My kind and straightforward therapist helped by constantly reminding me that just because my upbringing was so "good" that didn't mean I wasn't allowed to feel pain. That it was okay to feel grateful *and* resentful.

In the months to come, I allowed myself to do something I had never allowed myself to do before: share what I really felt.

I felt more and more relief. I would come back to the office with red blotches all over my face after my therapy appointment. Linda respected what little privacy we had between us and didn't ask.

I began to see how I had always dismissed my feelings to please, placate, delight. *Don't Feel Sorry for Yourself. Don't feel. And Good Lord you're too much. Tone it down.* I intuitively knew I was going to keep clocking through men, that I was never going to be able to have a real relationship, until I accepted all of me. Until I gave myself permission to feel *everything* and start to believe that I wasn't too much. I was deserving of love.

That was the year I started running, felt my feelings for the first time, and finally quit smoking once and for all.

CHAPTER SIX

"What you accomplish matters, but who you look at in the mirror every day matters most." - Dad

That next fall, my parents invited Molly and me to meet them at the Grand Canyon for a few days. Molly had moved to San Francisco, and we now lived a block away from each other. We jumped at the chance to take time off from our jobs and to see our parents.

On the ride back to the Phoenix airport, my mother was in the front seat next to my dad who was driving. Innocently, as if she was looking for something to talk about, asked, "Are you two going to church?"

Like a deer in a headlight, I froze. I thought to myself, *Oh God, what are you going to say?*

My sister mumbled, "Yeah, from time-to-time."

With a furrowed brow, she looked at Molly in the back seat and then her hazel eyes darted towards me. She snapped, "What about you?"

Fuck it, I thought. *It's time.* As matter of factly as I could muster,

I snarled, "No, I'm not."

In the rear-view mirror, I could see my dad's face flush red. He was known to keep his cool but this time he raised his voice and yelled out towards me, "What do you mean you don't go to church?!"

I would have jumped back to another row if I could have but we were sitting in a sedan. The car was starting to slow down as we approached the airport. I wasn't sure if he was just going to drop me off and keep driving.

I felt something stir in my gut. Instead of my usual instinct to retreat, I stayed with it just like I was learning in therapy. The stirring got bigger and bigger until, like a pressure cooker with no top, I couldn't hold it in any longer.

Instead of absorbing his disappointment, I roared back, "I don't know what more you could want from me! I'm doing God's work! That is what you taught me to do!" I surprised myself with the reference to God.

My dad and I didn't look at each other as I got out of the car. I sat in front of our gate back to San Francisco and cried with Molly all over my chicken tortilla soup. My tears weren't the weepy kind; they were spilling down my cheeks and filled with hot rage.

****

Two weeks later, I was sitting in my office at Summer Search. I had just talked with a student encouraging him to talk with his father about how he felt. Here I was pushing this student to take a risk and I had unfinished business with my own dad. I hung up, looked at the phone and thought, *What about you, Katherine?*

I dialed my dad's office line. He picked up on the first ring and greeted me with *'Joe Calihan'* in his signature strong voice.

"Hi, Dad."

"Champus [the special name he called me] how are you?" he asked with what felt like genuine curiosity.

I dismissed the warmth in his tone and leaned into the receiver, "I'm sorry that I've disappointed you. I'm sorry I don't go to church," my heart pounded through each word, "but I needed to tell you the truth."

I sat there listening to my own heartbeat. He didn't step into the silence, and I didn't either.

He was the first to speak. "Okay, well, I can't say I agree with your choices but at this stage in your life, you are free to make them." He hesitated and then went on, "The thing I don't understand is how angry you seem. What are you so angry about?"

Ack! He could see through me. My heartbeat was racing faster now. My invisible dukes were up. I was seething.

The adrenaline pumping through my limbs was gaining speed, but I took a second to gather my thoughts and blurted out, "All the work I've done listening to students has made me want to learn more about myself. It seems like all us pleasers stuff down too many feelings. I think I'm angry about a lot of things. One is that I feel like we don't even really know each other!"

Another awkward silence filled the airwaves. "I don't know what to say," he responded.

The phone lines started ringing, "Dad, I have to go."

We hung up with the sense that neither one of us knew what to do. Maybe the gulf between us was what it was. *Did he still love me?*

My heart knew he did. My mind wasn't so sure.

CHAPTER SEVEN

"People who can express themselves live a happier life." - Dad

A year later, it was a crisp November day. We were on South Drive, the house where I grew up in Pittsburgh. My family and I were standing around the kitchen island ripping apart stale bread the night before Thanksgiving so my mom could make the stuffing for the 22lb turkey the next day.

"I have an idea," my dad announced, "It's something we've never done before."

My dad wasn't seated at the head of the table, but it felt like he was as he casually continued, "As you may know, in 1976, I joined the *Young Presidents Organization*. That year, they sent me for training to learn how to run a peer-to-peer group called *'Forum.'* I started the first one here and have been part of the same group ever since. We've been meeting once or twice a year for over two decades. And I must add that the people in my forum are my closest confidantes."

I stood there listening genuinely happy that he had people in his life he could confide in.

Then he continued, "I'm thinking when we get together next time the six of us could have a forum meeting of our own. We'll set aside time together early in the day. I think it's a good way to connect, *outside of cocktail hour*. We can call them Family Meetings. Would you all be up for this?"

I was shocked but not entirely surprised. Even though my dad seemed to stay away from feelings, he was always curious about people's behavior. Maybe this was his attempt to put some focus on what was going on underneath the surface for each of us. I was secretly thrilled.

We all nodded and agreed that *'family meetings'* sounded like a good idea.

My mom smiled at him and then chimed in as she so often did, "Who would like another glass of wine?"

****

That spring, we gathered in the Bahamas in a place called Treasure Cay, a small community of expats and retirees looking for a low-key casual alternative to Florida. The water was jaw dropping-ly beautiful, but the real charm of the place was there wasn't much to do.

We sat in the living room on the pastel-colored couches of the condo where my parents now spent the winter months. I brought a pad of paper just in case.

My dad kicked it off, "I'd like this to be a confidential space where each of us will have the chance to speak for 10 minutes or so. You can talk about whatever you choose. It's a personal check-in. My hope is that over time you will use this time as a place to share what's really going on."

My dad was always in charge, but I had never quite seen him lead like this before.

I was learning through my work at Summer Search how to help others open up and share their feelings. Linda and I even used the same words to describe the conversations with our students: *check-*

ins. I was in awe that this was happening in my own family.

Yet that first time when it came my turn to speak, I didn't know what to say. I said a few things about Linda and Summer Search. *They don't want to hear about Linda and Summer Search.* I said a few things about biking across the Golden Gate Bridge. *They don't care what you do in your free time, Katherine.* I met a guy. *We've heard this before, Katherine.* My voice quivered, my eyes darted and by the time I finished, I *knew* I had taken too much space. I always did.

I don't remember what each of my siblings said. Most of it was a chorus of, *'Everything is good!'* It was the way we always talked despite this unique format. Even my mother's turn was brief as she looked to my father for his thoughts.

Getting us to open up might prove a little harder than he thought.

CHAPTER EIGHT

"Nothing worth having comes easy." - Dad

The night I met my future husband, he didn't see me at first; he heard me laughing. He asked the host of the party to introduce him to the person producing the sound of that baby calf cackle.

I was standing on the make-shift dance floor of the Victorian in the Haight Ashbury District of San Francisco when the host approached me with an extremely tall guy. As he walked over, I immediately noticed his height and his JFK, Jr boyish face. I also couldn't help but notice his chiseled biceps through his button down. I was drawn to his good looks, but I saw a kindness in the warmth of his face. He stood with his long legs wide apart like an easel so he could lean down to my 5'6" frame to introduce himself to me without having to hunch.

His name was Duncan. We talked about triathlons, the perks of living in the Bay Area and shared our pride in being from the east coast. We danced. He knew how to do *the pretzel!* He made me laugh. Sparks flew.

At the end of the night, when he didn't ask for my number, I dismissed my disappointment and turned with indignation to a friend and declared, *"He's too tall anyway!"* I had thrown myself on more men than I'd *still* like to admit and was finally starting to see how I was getting what I wanted—attention—but from men who weren't my equal or were just plain disinterested. I wanted a man who was strong enough to make the first move. I had had enough.

That Monday when the phone rang and the voice on the other line announced, "Hi, this is Duncan Kennedy. May I speak with Katherine?" I giggled and, without missing a beat, asked, "How did you get my number?"

"I looked it up in the phone book. You didn't realize it, but I was taking notes."

Oh...he must have felt it, too.

****

Our first date was my 27th birthday. He picked me up in a rusted dark maroon Chevy Tahoe. When I lifted myself into the seat of his truck, he handed me a card with bees on the cover and a sweet note inside about celebrating my birthday together. We sat across from each other at the Universal Cafe in a part of town called SOMA. I couldn't help but notice his slim fingers cupping a surprisingly short glass of Pilsner and wanted to kiss those lips of his that looked so juicy and inviting.

We found ourselves talking about our work, our lives, our upbringing, and being the babies of our families. We each had three older siblings. Our shared birth order alone made me think we might know exactly what the other experienced.

Later that night, I stood on a phone book to kiss him in front of my apartment overlooking the Bay. I asked him to come upstairs with me, and we laughed and kissed and stayed awake all night long. I was proud of myself for managing not to have sex that first night, but it happened soon enough. We couldn't keep our hands off each other.

After just one week, as we danced to *Crazy Love* by Van Morrison in my apartment, he admitted he was falling in love with me. I tilted my neck to be able to lock eyes with him and froze.

The only words that came out were, "I know."

This is all you have been working towards, Katherine. A real relationship with an incredible guy who makes you laugh. What is wrong with you?

This time, shame, that mean voice in my head, didn't put me in a spiral of self-loathing. Instead, I woke up the next morning, drove over to his apartment, and found him reading a Harlan Coben novel in bed. I nestled in and admitted that I loved him.

"I'm sorry I didn't say what I was really feeling last night," I owned.

"I know it's scary," he reassured me, stretching his long arm around my back, "I'm scared, too."

****

My parents welcomed Duncan into our house over Thanksgiving and rolled out the red carpet. The red carpet, of course, was the color of the rug in the basement where my mother set up a temporary bed. She put a picture of me from kindergarten on a little night table. It was ten years after the 'incident' with Greg but separate bedrooms before marriage was the Catholic way. When I asked my mother why she welcomed Duncan so graciously into our home after hearing about so many other men over the years, she said she could tell it in my voice. It also helped that after our first date I announced, "I think he's the one, Mom."

Six months later, after a 6-mile run together in the hills of the Marin Headlands, Duncan got down on his knee, pulled out a ring from a bulky little green box that had somehow been hidden in his pocket, and asked me to marry him. "*Let's take on life together,*" he said. I screamed "*Yes!*" with delight, and we sat on a bench overlooking Sausalito with our bodies wrapped into one.

Six months after that, Duncan began his toast at the rehearsal dinner delighting, "They broke the mold when they made Katherine." Everyone rejoiced. Finally, a man who understood her!

At our wedding reception on Treasure Island in the middle of the San Francisco Bay, our priest didn't stick around after cocktails, so I ran up to my Dad and asked him to give the blessing. Without hesitation, he grabbed the microphone and thanked everyone for being there. He acknowledged the union of two families and the hope that Duncan and I would have the joy of knowing our children's children.

I asked the 3-piece quartet who were playing during cocktail hour to kick off the night with any song of their choosing for my dad and me. Picking a father/daughter song was one detail I forgot. If I was mentoring myself, I would have commented, *"That's interesting Katherine. What do you think that's about?"*

The band played an instrumental version of *Somewhere* by Barbara Streisand. As we danced, I knew I hit the jackpot being one of Joe Calihan's daughters, but our dance still felt a little bit forced. Something was still missing. I secretly agreed with Streisand's words and longed for the moment that someday, somewhere there would be a time for us, too.

****

The worst floods since 1896 hit the southern island where Duncan and I were in New Zealand for our honeymoon, so we cut our losses and flew home early. When we landed at SFO, I didn't dare report back early to work or call anyone. I just wanted to be stuck like glue to my new husband.

Throughout our first year of marriage, we worked, we trained for triathlons, we watched movies together, we fell asleep in each other's arms and woke up in the same position in the morning. I had never been happier.

When Duncan and I traveled to Kauai to celebrate our first anniversary, I assumed we would have sex morning, noon, and night. Turns out this place for honeymooners is where I discovered ours was over!

Duncan seemed to have other visions of our vacation. I had

never been to Hawaii. I was bursting with enthusiasm but when we sat on the plane, Duncan engrossed himself in his Newsweek. When we arrived at the Princeville Hotel, Duncan changed into his bathing suit and headed down to the pool. I shuffled down to the pool behind him.

As he drifted into his own inner world, I reacted by using the same coping mechanisms I used as a child when I felt lonely, and when I told myself that no one cared or was paying any attention. I tried to charm; to get a laugh. It didn't work. He didn't laugh, he wasn't as interested in small talk or, it seemed, in me. I didn't know if this was normal, I didn't know what to do. Stomping around him didn't seem to work, either! I quickly talked myself out of what I was feeling, brushed my fears aside and focused on the fact that we were in Hawaii, for goodness sakes, and that we were building a life together. And for a while, that dream was enough.

****

We decided to start trying to have a baby the following summer. Duncan was so ready to be a dad that he held me up by the ankles after we made love to conceive. It must have worked because when I went to Safeway to buy a pregnancy test, I let out a *terrified-and-excited-all-at-the-same-time* scream when the stick told me I was pregnant.

Charlie arrived on Mother's Day. The day we brought him home from the hospital was the scariest day of my life. This little bundle of life was in our hands. My heart was swooning with love, but my head was full of anxiety.

My earliest days of parenting him were full of reveling in smiles and his earliest words. I had never experienced a love so visceral, so profound. Yet everything felt like an emergency. Duncan tried to be helpful, yet I found myself agreeing with the title of a book I stumbled upon called, *I Wish My Husband was My House Cleaner*. I started to wonder why marriage as an institution even existed. He couldn't think two steps ahead. *He's not a mind reader, Katherine. He's not a nurse,* I told myself.

49

Duncan and I thought we wanted four children like the families we were raised in but changed our minds after our second child came along. We named him Joey after my dad. Joey was sleeping through the night and couldn't have been an easier baby—but still—we turned to each other exhausted one early morning and confirmed, *"How about just one more?"*

Two years later, the doctor told me my third child would be a girl and I screamed, *"I'm afraid!"* on the sonogram table. I was finally a confident mother of two boys. I knew how to wrestle, poke, and play with Charlie and Joey on the floor. A daughter was going to give me a new challenge of modeling how to be a strong, confident woman. If the story I told myself was rooted in shame, how was I going to be able to pass down a different narrative? I had my doubts.

Underneath that fear was a persistent belief that I didn't deserve the blessing of a daughter. How could I possibly ask from life anything more than what I already had? All that said, we welcomed Kate (named after me) with open arms.

Seven years into our marriage, we were living the dream in the fog belt of San Francisco in a green Edwardian with a purple princess tree in front. It was a joyful, sweet time with so much laughter in our home.

But soon after Kate was born, our sex life disappeared. Our three healthy children and fulfilling careers were more than enough to fill in the space of the growing distance between us. *Don't feel sorry for yourself,* I told myself. I didn't know what to do.

****

It was like any other day. The frantic rush of grocery shopping, email checking, throwing toys in the color-coded bins for the millionth time. I was alone, or at least I felt that way. And if I wasn't going to feel in control of my life, well, guess what, n*either was he.*

Duncan walked in from his day job and put his papers down as he walked into the kitchen. "That's mine!" I screamed. "How could you put your stuff down where my stuff is? You just went ahead and put your computer there even though mine was already there. And look! You've used my notebook!"

Why are you making such a big deal over that spot? It's a desk for God's sake. Who cares where he puts his stuff down? I heard those voices question my reaction to him but that didn't stop me.

"Fuck you!" came barreling out of my mouth.

To my surprise, Duncan did a double take, looked down the stairs to the TV room to make sure the kids were watching Scooby Doo, and with steely and pointed eyes at me, screamed back,

"NO... Fuck YOU!"

The words were dark, but I could almost hear the balloon popping releasing all the hostility and built-up tension from our bodies. As we stood there, unsure of what to do next, a relieved little voice inside of me whispered: *You made contact.*

A couple nights after the *Fuck You* showdown, we stood in the bathroom side by side brushing our teeth.

I looked at him in the double sized mirror and, over the buzz of my Sonicare, I announced, "I think we should see someone. You know, a therapist. It's time to mourn your mother and I don't know how to help you."

Duncan's mother had been diagnosed with a cancer that had spread so much that the doctors weren't sure where it started. Her death a couple months before didn't seem to rock the family or my husband. This scared me. At the rate I was going, Duncan might be relieved if I wasn't around as well.

"And I don't know what's going on between us," I added like an afterthought.

Duncan was cupping water from the faucet and rinsing his

mouth. "I'm afraid of what I might find out," he responded ever so quietly.

I didn't know what he didn't want to find out, but I knew that I was scared, too. I didn't know what was going to be uncovered. Like his mom's cancer, I couldn't name exactly where or why our problems started either. Was there someone else? Was he even sad about losing his mom? *Did he still love me?*

Instead of responding, I acted like I couldn't hear him, finished brushing my teeth, and went to bed.

CHAPTER NINE

"Never assume you know what someone is thinking." - Dad

When Duncan and I sat down on the therapist's couch I couldn't help but notice the tattered seams and frayed white strings reminding me there had been others before us.

"Where do you want to begin?" Jeb, the therapist, asked.

We looked at each other. I felt an overwhelming urge to talk about our dwindling sex life and the dynamic we fell into at our worst. How I barked as he retreated. But I sat there quietly. I had learned from interviewing students to not fill in the space.

Duncan started talking about his mother dying and my suggestion to see a therapist.

"What do you remember about her?" Jeb asked.

"I was the baby. I always felt like I had a special place in her heart. But a fork would drop, and she'd launch into a fit of rage," he hesitated and then added, "I tried to stay out of her way."

He shared a few random stories with no apparent connection. Then there was a long silence in the room. "I don't know what else to say," Duncan admitted.

After a brief pause, Jeb asked, "How interested are you in finding out more about your mother?"

Duncan looked at me and shrugged, "I've made it here, why not."

Jeb gave us homework. He encouraged Duncan to talk with his father and learn more about his parents' marriage. The more we could learn, the better we could see what we were bringing to the table, he assured us.

****

When Duncan's father visited us weeks later, we took him out to dinner at *The Cliff House,* looking out over the Pacific Ocean. As the light faded from the sky, we ate oysters and shellfish. Duncan and I gave each other the nod, signaling it was time to get the conversation started.

"Dad, Katherine and I wanted to ask you a few questions about Mom."

Mike nodded and looked at us both through what we called his coke-bottle glasses.

"Can you first tell your dad why, Duncan?" I suggested.

"Oh yeah, sure. Katherine and I started to see a therapist about a month ago. We haven't been communicating as well as we think we can be and so we reached out for help. He suggested we have this conversation with you."

His father responded with his almost British-sounding accent reserved for people raised on the Upper East Side of Manhattan, "That sounds like a wonderful idea."

I piped in, "Thank you, Mike. We've prepared a list of questions." Like an attorney about to take a deposition, I pulled out a yellow manila pad of paper with the first page full of questions as I searched in my purse for a pen. Once my fingers found one, I looked at them both and announced, "Okay, we're ready."

Duncan had been told he had a temper growing up. My experience in our marriage was closer to Duncan holding it all in. We couldn't put our finger on it, but the stories did not align. So naturally, his first question to his dad wasn't about his mom, it was about himself.

"Dad, I was told I had a temper, but I don't really remember that. What was I like as a kid?"

Mike paused and folded the white napkin on his lap.

"Duncan, what you have to understand is that you were born into a very unhappy marriage," he calmly volunteered.

The words felt like blinding rays of sun beaming on us. Bright and hard to absorb. I knew my husband grew up trying to avoid his mother's toxic rage, but I hadn't realized the context. I only heard the *she-was-crazy* story, never the *they-were-unhappy* story. I thought, *fifty-three years is a long time to be unhappy.*

"What do you mean?" Duncan asked with a curious tone.

"Well as you know, I was in captivity in Tehran [my father-in-law was one of the 52 hostages in 1980 and wrote a book about being in captivity for 444 days]. And I wasn't sure if I would return home to your mother. Even if I was freed. As a kid, Duncan you were on your own. I'm not quite sure you had the temper you've been told. I think it was your mother who had one."

No wonder Duncan kept tiptoeing around me. He probably spent his childhood trying to avoid any eruption of anger, to keep the peace, to try and make her happy.

She must have been lonely, I thought. I had never made the connection between lashing out with loneliness. I scribbled *rage=loneliness* and kept going down the list.

We continued to ask questions and listen to Mike open up about what he experienced both in his marriage and growing up. At the end of the evening, Duncan and I walked hand in hand to the car knowing we had just done something courageous.

That night when we got into bed, I looked at him and grinned, "I'm proud of you, Duncan, for asking those questions. I'm proud of your dad for being so honest. And...I'm proud of us...for doing this *together.*"

****

One day the therapist quipped, "Katherine, you're like the Bette Davis character who holds a cigarette in one hand and a drink in the other while complaining about her hard life. Why do you think this is happening?" Every time we were showing up to therapy, we without fail had some conflict the night before or the day of. It was like we were priming ourselves.

I pictured a shriveled up maudlin character in a light pink silk bathrobe swaying through her black and white marbled ballroom. The cigarette was in her right hand and burning at the end of a holder. In her left hand, a green pimiento olive is rolling around in her martini, spilling, as she stumbled through her mansion all alone.

The visual was unnerving.

'I prefer margaritas, not martinis,' I wanted to say but thought the joke could be interpreted as defensive. I was no stranger to using humor to deflect deeper feelings but had a sense it could be perceived as sarcasm. Sarcasm always felt a little hostile to me.

"Be the person you want to be, Katherine," my mother's words rang in my ear again.

We now knew that Duncan was distancing himself to keep from escalating any eruption of anger in me. I had been interpreting his need for distance as a punishment, his need for solitude as a rejection. The pain of what felt like isolation caused an endless loop of negative thoughts about him...and me. *Something must be wrong with me. He must not still love me.* The old story was gaining momentum.

Instead of expressing how hurt, sad, or disillusioned I was feeling, I became the Bette Davis character or worse, Duncan's mother when the fork fell. Instead of asking for what I needed: help, love, touch, closeness, I found ways to push him away further. I lashed out. *Rage=loneliness.* It was showing up in our marriage, too.

Why was it so hard for me to ask for what I needed? What was playing out from my own background? I wondered. Could it be related to the unspoken tension between my parents when I was in high school? Or maybe I was feeling the loneliness of my upbringing, when I tried to hide all my feelings inside and pretend everything was okay? I was bringing more baggage to the relationship than I wanted to admit. One thing was for certain: keeping everything inside had only made things worse.

I kept pushing Duncan away and he kept walking on eggshells around me. It was exhausting for us both.

****

The awareness helped but didn't solve everything. When Duncan and I showed up to therapy the following month, Jeb began the session with his usual invitation, "Let's evolve!"

But I was in no mood to evolve. I was mad at Duncan for leaving me feeling stranded during the kid's bedtime routine the night before.

Jeb invited us to sit on the floor.

I was about to roll my eyes at another *Northern Californian* therapy technique when I saw my husband slide his nearly seven-foot frame onto the worn oriental carpet, cross his long legs and look up at me. I stood from the couch and joined him.

"I'd like you to just look at each other," Jeb requested. "For three minutes."

I looked away and almost let my baby calf cackle out. I stopped myself when I saw Duncan looking at me.

His eyes were soft and present. I told myself, *Don't pull away. He's with you, Katherine. He's here.*

Three minutes felt like an eternity.

In his blue eyes I could see him for maybe the first time in our 10-year marriage. I could see the little boy who had to retreat to survive. I could see the young man who tried to take care of everyone and keep the peace. I could see the weathered middle-aged man choosing to still love me.

And I could see through the tears that were trickling down both of our faces that we were still in it, together. In that moment, we didn't need words. The sparks were everywhere.

CHAPTER TEN

"Trust your instincts." - Dad

"When will you be able to talk with your dad, Katherine?" Jeb asked.

I felt affronted. My family was so much more *functional*. Although, when I mentioned the year before at a family meeting that Duncan and I were in therapy, no one commented. There was dead silence in fact. I felt vulnerable and exposed.

We'd been having family meetings for over a decade now. Each one of us was getting more and more honest about our struggles. Being given the space to talk, be listened to, with no interruptions or cross talk had been a game changer. Our spouses were a part of the annual meetings as my parents felt they were as much a part of the family as the original six of us. The meetings were starting to feel like a kind of glue that kept us from growing distant.

But of course, I knew Jeb was right.

My dad had announced in that same meeting that he wanted to take each of his adult children away on a trip. He thought the one-on-one time could be special. His priorities had shifted a bit. He and my mom had very little interest in mindlessly traveling in their older age. They wanted to devote their extra time and travel to experiences with us. He was also thinking of starting a nonprofit in honor of his grandfather. He wanted to help entrepreneurs from under resourced neighborhoods to get the skills and support they needed to succeed.

I waited my turn for a trip and knew one-on-one time was the opportunity to dive in with him and ask him about the things that I'd kept to myself growing up. I was nervous. Could I be myself with him? What if he got to really know me and didn't like what he saw? If he got to know me, *would he still love me?*

It had been 20 years since he saw me in bed as a teenager with that camp-counselor-boyfriend. It had been 10 years since the ride to the airport in Arizona. I was building a life in San Francisco as a mother, a wife and successful nonprofit executive. We'd had many fun times together, so many in fact. He was an incredible man. *Why couldn't I just let the past go?*

We met at Molly's house in Los Gatos, a sunny suburb of San Jose, to drive together down the California coast in a bright red rental car to Santa Barbara. Google maps had just hit the scene, telling us it would take six hours. *Would we run out of things to talk about?* I wondered.

Driving down the winding roads of Route 1, I noticed something new about him. He would ask open ended questions, like the way Linda had taught me in mentoring the students. Lots of *'Tell me about...'* which gave me the open space to share anything. His curiosity made me feel so comfortable. Maybe he always had been that way, maybe I had just never really noticed. Or maybe we just hadn't had a chance to focus on each other. By then there were 14 grandchildren, and the family gatherings were becoming more and more of a whirlwind every time.

The next morning, we parked on the main drag of Santa Barbara and walked side by side along the sun-drenched manicured street. I thought it would be easier to have the conversation if we were walking, and not sitting across from each other.

I felt the muscles around my heart clench. It was time. I closed my mouth to be able to breathe in through my nose and calm my nerves. I kept my eyes on the perfect pattern of concrete blocks along the sidewalk.

"You know how at our last family meeting Duncan and I opened up about seeing a therapist?"

I felt my face flush. I still couldn't help but be embarrassed about that.

"Well anyway, my point is that because of this work, we are really trying to look at our upbringings in a deeper way and address some things we have swept under the rug. Can I talk to you about a couple of things that happened growing up?"

He responded with genuine openness, "Sure."

I continued, "When you caught me in bed when I was 17 with Greg, you didn't look or talk with me for several months. Can I ask you...What was that about?"

I wasn't sure who skipped breathing first, him or me. We kept walking but turned our heads slightly towards each other.

He was quiet for a second. "You know, Katherine, I parented you kids from a very strict sense of right and wrong. And I think I felt like I failed as a parent," he speculated pensively.

I listened and didn't say anything. He continued,

"We probably should have gotten some help. When my brother died, I never talked about how it impacted me. I'm pretty sure the tremor I've struggled with in my right hand since I was a kid has to do with that loss. I've never felt sorry for myself, but it's taken me a long time to learn about how my feelings have impacted me. That we feel better when we share them."

I didn't say anything but was right there with him, hanging on to every word and step we were taking together.

He went on, "That was a hard time as a father and as a husband. I was upset with you, but I was also upset with myself. And your mother and I at that time weren't on the same page. I wasn't sure what to do."

The way he said it put me right there with him. I wasn't sure what I would have done either.

I acknowledged what was being said, "Yeah, that was hard Dad. I wish we would have gotten help. I have to say I've focused for so long on how much your reaction hurt me that I'm embarrassed I've never really thought about how much it must have crushed you."

I added, "I wish you had looked at me, though."

We were two blocks away from the car, so I knew I needed to find my courage to ask my second question. He had just alluded to some hard times in their marriage. *You can do this, Katherine. You're not in trouble.* I heard a voice inside scream, *Are you going to fucking step up or regret this for the rest of your life?*

"Hey Dad. There's one more thing." I reminded myself the shaking in my glute was just fear.

"Sure, what is it?"

"When I was thirteen, I heard you in the den talking on the phone with someone. From the tone of your voice, I don't think it was Mom. I'm sorry to bring this up but I've wondered about it my whole life and never had the courage to ask."

We had started to slow down our steps, but now, he stopped in his tracks. His eyes widened and he turned his head to the left towards me as if to ask a question.

"There was a woman. She was from Charlotte. Gosh, what was her name?"

His lack of defensiveness caught me off guard. There was not even a hint of it.

My head turned to him, but I didn't dare look at his face. I felt a rush of joy. *You did it. You did it. You did it, Katherine. You asked the hardest question.* My heart was beating fast, beaming with joy.

It almost didn't matter what he said next.

"She worked at the Charlotte office. When I would travel, she was always so happy to see me. Your mother was always mad. Mad at what I didn't do. Mad at what I didn't say. Mad the minute I walked through the door. We weren't communicating well."

I thought, *I bet she was. I can't imagine Duncan playing golf every Saturday after being gone all week. I'd be irate.* But I didn't say anything. I did what I had now learned to do. I waited.

And because I waited, because I was *listening to understand,* not listening so I could have my turn to speak, blame or be heard, I learned what it was like to be in his shoes.

"Having that attention was tempting. And yeah, it was a hard moment of time in our marriage, but I just couldn't do it. Your mother was the only woman I have ever loved."

We realized we had unconsciously stopped right in front of the rental car. We looked at the car and at each other and without words motioned with our eyes that it was time to get in.

My dad got in the driver's seat, I sat in the passenger seat and together we drove up a 10-mile winding road into the San Ysidro Valley.

He continued, "I don't know if I have ever told you, but I went and saw a therapist for six months many years ago. I discovered just how devastated I was by the loss of my brother. I became a people pleaser to not risk losing anyone's love again."

I listened; I shared more about what was playing out with Duncan and he talked candidly about some of his challenges during those years. I think we both gave a sigh of relief as we understood exactly what the other one was saying.

For the first time in my whole life, I could see my father, not just as a larger-than-life character I grew up with but a man, a human on a journey to heal and change and grow. I think he saw that in me, too.

CHANGE

CHAPTER ELEVEN

"Keep it simple, stupid." – Dad

I was sitting in a school counselor's office. It felt eerily like the ones I used to interview students all those years ago when I worked at *Summer Search*. It had been five years since I left my job and 10 years since that walk in Santa Barbara with my dad.

I was now running my own coaching business. People, mostly adults, came to me for help crafting their story, preparing for a TED talk, or giving a toast. Yet this day, a nonprofit hired me to work with a teenager named Carlos and help him prepare to tell his story for their annual fundraiser.

The phone was buzzing, and I caught a glance at the screen announcing *Papa* calling. I don't usually look at my phone in the middle of coaching, let alone answer it, but it was March 1st, my dad's 81st birthday. If I didn't pick up, with the three-hour time difference, I might have missed my chance to wish him a Happy Birthday.

My dad's voice sounded heavy and more serious than usual so I asked Carlos if I could pop out and talk with him. I walked into the hallway and sat on a wooden bench that had a sign spelling 'DREAM BIG' above it.

"How are you doing, Dad?" I asked.

"Well, the fatigue I've been experiencing has been caused by a blockage in the valve between the liver and the pancreas. They believe that it's a tumor. We'll know more in the coming days after I get a CT scan."

My heart sank. I sat motionless and stared into space. To gather my composure, I took a big inhale and exhaled, stood up, and walked back into the counselor's office where Carlos was still sitting. I knew I was going to do something I had never done with a client before. I looked at him and whispered, "My dad just told me he might have cancer. Do you mind if we meet next week?"

Two days later, I was sitting in a full-size black coach bus with the basketball team's parents heading up to Sacramento to watch my oldest son Charlie and his classmates play in the California State Championships. Everyone was busy chatting, and the bus was humming up I-80 when I saw *Papa* appear on my iPhone again. I put the phone up to my ear and heard both my mom and dad say in unison, "Hi Katherine."

My dad said, "We have some things we need to talk to you about, but it sounds like this isn't a good time. Why don't you call us tomorrow?" Before I had much of any chance to respond, they hung up.

Tomorrow? *Are you kidding me?* I screamed inside. I didn't know anything but what I did know was that it probably wasn't good news. I called Molly. She didn't pick up. I called Anne. She didn't pick up. I called Marty's wife, Jenni. I tried texting. Nothing. The chatter on the bus took a back seat as I grasped Duncan's arm and started to heave. It was the beginning of the end; my body knew it.

The bus stopped at an intersection with a mixture of one-story houses and broken up sidewalks. I tuned out the words *Sandra Dee's* written across the restaurant on the corner where the other parents filed off the bus and inside to order her famous barbeque. I had no idea where I was as I stood on the sidewalk and called my dad's cell. He picked up.

"Okay Katherine, I hear you've been trying to reach us and understand I need to tell you what is going on." I gripped the phone harder.

"The tumor was stage IV and deep in the pancreas. It's inoperable." His voice was clear but somber.

I paced and couldn't stop.

"I also have cancer in my lungs although they are not certain it is the same cancer. I have a 50% chance of living one more year. But we just don't know."

I struggled for words. I had spent my whole life trying to find my dad and now he was about to be taken away from me.

****

As soon as I got home, I packed my bags. There was one place I wanted to be. I found a ticket leaving Saturday night and within 36 hours of hearing the news, I jumped on a plane with Molly to meet my mom, Dad, Marty, and Anne in the Bahamas where we had gathered many years before.

Molly and I got to my parents' bungalow before them. I had just walked out of the bathroom when I heard the gravel. *They must be here,* I thought. I braced myself as I heard the screen door slam like it always did.

I didn't know what to expect.

But the man who walked through the door looked just like my dad. Radiant. Big smile. Arms wide open. He wore a white button down with his glasses held by a strap on his chest. Nothing had changed.

"How are you?" he asked. "Better now!" I exclaimed. I was determined to keep it together.

He stood there in the middle of the kitchen, as if he was holding court. He exclaimed, "I cannot tell you what this means to me to have you all drop everything and be here. I think we have a real opportunity to process this together. I want everything to be put on the table and nothing left unsaid."

Despite the heaviness in my heart, I sat there watching my dad surprised by a feeling of lightness in my chest. What I thought would be fear was actually a kind of joy. Over the past several years I had set up monthly calls with my dad. I asked questions about all matters of life and work. We had traveled together two more times. Once to Boulder and the other time to New York City.

I had asked for closeness. My dad delivered.

****

There in the Bahamas, we were the original six: Dad, Mom, Marty, Anne, Molly, and me. We began our process of dealing with the fact that our dad would die. And he was there to remind us and our fears that everything was going to be okay.

"Let's enjoy this time together. One thing you need to know is that I'm not afraid of dying," he added.

Lunch hours turned into long afternoons sitting around the table overlooking the light blue water reminiscing, sharing, asking questions. The wine flowed every evening, and we asked more questions and listened to every word. We swam in stories of my dad's upbringing and never felt closer.

On the third morning, my dad suggested we each take a walk with him separately out to a small stretch of beach where the tides came together known as *The Point*. We had spent hours there year after year looking for sand dollars. My dad and I took our flip flops off and hid them in the dunes by a light pink house as we headed for the crystal blue water.

"How are you doing Dad? You seem so strong," I said.

"You know Katherine, how I am sounding is really how I'm feeling. My own parents showed me the way towards approaching the end of their life, and I hope that someday this will help you, too."

"Dad, you've lived your life without regret, so you get to die without regret. It's incredible to me."

As the tears streamed down my face, I added, "You've shown me so many lessons, but this is what you are showing me now."

We stood there with the water hitting our ankles, looking right at each other. I told him how grateful I was. I told him that the close relationship we created was everything to me. I wasn't sure if he had something to tell me. I was nervous but soldiered on, "Is there something you want to tell me?"

He looked at me with his twinkling brown eyes, "You might recall the story about the first time your mother and I got in a fight. I asked her if she still loved me, and she said, "*Love has nothing to do with it.*" I hope one day you will tell your kids the '*Do-you-still-love-me' story.*' I hope you've learned you can never really know what is going on in someone's head unless you ask. And Katherine, please, don't assume that they are rejecting you."

And then he assured me, "I know you love me, Champus."

****

A couple months later, another shoe dropped even closer to home. My son Charlie and I were walking up to our house in San Francisco after taking a Lyft home from the airport. We had just come back from a college visit on the east coast and stopped in Pittsburgh to see my mom and dad. My dad had started chemo and spent most of the two days while we were there on the couch. He laid on his back with the TV remote in his hand, feeling overwhelming fatigue.

Before I had a chance to get the key out of my purse, Duncan swung open the front door and barged out on the blue stone entryway. Before we even made eye contact, he blurted out, "I have a tumor."

My body jerked backwards. My eyes blinked for what felt like an eternity. It was like deja vu. Only six weeks before my dad told me he was dying with a tumor and now, my husband had one.

I heard a rumbling in my stomach. All I could think about suddenly was that I had only had two hard boiled eggs to eat all day.

"Okay, okay let's go upstairs and sit, and you can tell us everything."

I stopped in the kitchen and grabbed a handful of cashews. I had just come from witnessing my mom taking care of my dad. She was so strong. I knew I was going to need some strength of my own.

Duncan and I walked into the living room and sat down on the two swivel chairs. Charlie was just shy of 16 years old and positioned himself on the couch right in between us. I wasn't sure if he should be there, but I felt there was no turning back; we were in it together.

"Okay. Tell us everything," I said.

Duncan had a colonoscopy earlier in the week. The doctor on call found a three-inch tumor where the colon meets the rectum. The doctor recommended a surgeon we happened to know, and Duncan was able to schedule a CT scan that afternoon. Could I take him to the hospital?

For the two days I was with my parents, my father's diagnosis dominated every waking hour. I watched my mom deal with the impending loss of her husband by being present, attending to his needs, and infusing humor and all the jokes they had come to love between them. In that exact moment I thought, *Okay...I know what to do. Let's go get that scan.*

The distinction between the two cancers proved helpful. We could explain to the kids that while Papa's cancer was terminal, their dad's cancer was treatable. The outpouring of love from our friends was overwhelming and nourishing.

My parents kept reminding me to stay focused on Duncan. That it would do no good to worry about Papa. I heeded their advice. Even though I knew my dad had terminal cancer, I knew I wasn't just my dad's daughter in the world anymore. I was a mother and a wife. And my family needed me.

I started running again. Shuffling is probably a more accurate word, but I hadn't run since the kids were little. I started with a mile then built up to three. I knew I needed a healthy way to deal with the stress of it all. One morning I got to the top of a vista where I could see the Golden Gate Bridge and screamed with all my might, "Fuuuck!!!!" A guy ran by me and asked if I was okay. I didn't know anyone was there or where else to unleash all I was holding.

It was a long few months of the trifecta treatments of radiation, surgery and chemo. Duncan's stoicism and sense of humor worked to everyone's favor. I had never felt more anchored in what was important and where to put my energy and focus.

****

By March 1st of 2020, my dad had lived an entire year since his diagnosis. The chemo had stopped working before the holidays and he was now in a clinical trial. I went to visit him in Pittsburgh for his 82nd birthday, along with my mom and siblings. His spirits were so high, his energy so good, his coloring so effervescent, I almost thought he would live forever.

But, by the time I flew home to San Francisco and the lockdowns from COVID were in place, my dad's health abruptly took a turn for the worse. He went to the hospital, and they found cancer throughout his colon. He had a surgery to put in an ileostomy bag, and after a couple weeks of monitoring, the doctors said there were no more options. It was time to discharge him from the hospital and send him home to die in the comfort of his home.

My mother ushered in a hospital bed to the guest room along with a new understanding that the end would look very different than we originally thought. With COVID realities, a funeral wouldn't be likely. Certainly, no big reception. All we could ask for was what we had hoped for all along, that he wouldn't have to suffer.

I lost 70% of my business in the first few months of sheltering-in-place and turned my attention to working on something important for me to do while my dad was still alive: writing his eulogy. I wrote about his sayings. I wrote about his success in business. I wrote about our trips together. *'Imagine feeling from your own father that you are enough?'* When I wrote that one line, it hit me what an incredible thing he had given me: the gift of his unconditional love.

I texted him and asked him if I could share the eulogy I had written. He read it and texted me back, "How can a dad who loves his daughter not be blown away by your expressions of our lives together. I am so glad that I saw your message in its original form. I loved every part of it. Love, love, love, Dad."

When we talked the following day, he couldn't help but give me a few pointers. "Just focus on the relationship we created, Champus." He was right. It was all about the relationship.

****

A month later, my dad made the decision to stop eating and we knew what that meant. We were in the final stretch. In the wake of COVID, I chose not to jump on a plane. I asked my dad what he thought. He agreed it wasn't prudent. I think he and my mom appreciated their daily routine and last days together and I made peace with myself for not going to see him.

But our *Zoom* calls continued. In preparation for one call where we decided to reminisce about the good times, I brainstormed and wrote on a stack of bright pink post-it notes moments from a lifetime of family experiences. I put them up all over my dining room table. I wanted to be ready.

The next morning, I woke up and slid out of the house for a morning run up to the Golden Gate Bridge. As I ran across the street to a makeshift dirt path in the Presidio that led up the coastal trail, my thoughts were with my dad. I knew it was coming. I felt him with me, like a warm coat, enveloping me with care.

When I got back to the house, I looked at my phone and saw a family text from Marty that must have come in just minutes before. "Can you all FaceTime in five minutes? It is important. I will initiate."

I was the first one on. I realized as Marty and my mom appeared on the same screen together, that he was at my parents' place. I sat down at the table with all my pink post-it notes staring at me. When Molly and Anne joined in, Marty spoke.

"Dad died. It happened."

In unison my sisters cried out, "Oh My God!"

I quietly yelped. I leaned over my knees, closed my eyes and took a deep breath.

My mother chimed in, "Yes it just happened. And it happened so fast."

Marty continued, "The nurse was about to leave. She went to move his pillow and get him more comfortable when she realized what was going on. She told us he was passing." Marty paused, his eyes were welling up, "Mom got to hold him. It lasted for about 30 minutes."

The little FaceTime squares with our faces expanded and contracted. My mom's face was still as she spoke, "I was standing right there, and we looked at each other the whole time. He said, *I love you* and then I said, *I love you* back. He said, *God bless*, and I said, *God Bless* you back."

My mother paused and sniffled a bit and then said, "He looked at me and whispered *Amen* and then he died."

****

The funeral was scheduled for Memorial Day. Molly and I made our travel plans. We decided that our husbands and kids would stay back in California and could stream the service on Facebook Live. COVID continued to dominate our fears but some part of me was okay that we were going without them. This was my family, my father.

The service was at *Sacred Heart Church* in Pittsburgh. The Bishop of Pittsburgh was officiating and the whole strange scene felt entirely normal and complete. This was the church that we'd attended on Saturday nights as kids, this was the church my sister Anne was married in, this was the church that would have been filled to the brim with people who loved and admired my dad. When I walked in and saw the magnificent stained-glass windows and smelled the faint smell of incense, I felt at home again.

I was there with Marty, Anne, Molly, my mom and a handful of close relatives. Half of us carried my dad's casket down the middle aisle. Instead of proceeding to the front of the church with the gold enameled crucifix, we turned left into the chapel and positioned the casket at the foot of the little altar. The space was small and intimate and as I stepped into my pew 6 feet apart from Molly with my mask on, I couldn't help but feel grateful that it was just us.

I sat down in the church pew and looked at my mom who was right in front of me. She was sitting with her spine tall, but no doubt a heavy heart. She wore a navy-blue dress with a sash and a full skirt. Elegant as ever. I looked down at her hands, suddenly overcome by the fact that after 57 years of marriage my dad was able to die in the hands of the woman he loved.

I looked around at the few family members who were able to be there. It wasn't the number of people but the power of the love that felt so real and true. I felt as lucky as any person could ever hope to feel in the wake of losing their father.

We had loved each other, we had healed together, and, in the end, nothing had been left unsaid.

As I walked out of the church that day, there was only one word left.

Amen.

EPILOGUE

I wrote this story during COVID, and the creative process was like a dear friend during an unsettling time. It also helped me grieve the loss of my dear dad.

But let's face it, writing is hard. Part of the struggle came from my fear of sharing intimate details about myself and my family.

The other part was finding the words. I love *having written* this but putting words on paper can be excruciating, especially because of that mean voice that lives in so many of our heads that tells us we don't know how to write.

Just as I often tell my clients, I needed to take some of my own unique medicine throughout.

Trust the process, Katherine. I reminded myself to not worry about the outcome.

Challenge. Choice. Change. I followed my simple and unique framework.

Share what's inside. I had faith that the wisdom my story could teach others would reveal itself to me.

When my husband, mother and siblings read a pretty-close-to-final version, I heard, "*You nailed it...I'm proud of you...You've expressed yourself, Katherine,"* and I let out a sigh of relief. I wanted their validation *and* their approval, but I wasn't willing to forgo the truth to receive those things. I hoped that if I shared our imperfections that they would still love me. That vulnerable age-old question, 'Do-you-still-love-me' *still* pops up from time to time inside of me. I'm pretty sure they still do. *Thank goodness.*

To my surprise, however, when those rich and deep conversations wrapped up, I started to get even *more* anxious. Now what do I do? And should I have written more about my mom? What about Linda and what we created at Summer Search? What about Molly? What about Duncan? What about my kids? Other even more pesky negative thoughts of my own emerged like *Who do you think you are? You're way too much. Why on earth would you share this with anybody?* Oh, the stories I started to tell myself!

And now months later, I've wrestled enough with myself and decided to say my own version of *Fuck it.* Kind of like when I was in the car with my parents and spoke my truth. Sometimes that is the fuel we need to stand in our truth.

My dad instilled in me this idea to be in service in the world. His life shined bright and his words and his unconditional love lives inside of me every moment of every single day. I might not feel this way if I hadn't shared with him what was inside.

I'm sharing this story [as well as my struggle in telling it] in service of the idea that you'll be inspired to tell an important story of your own and discover the unique wisdom that your story can teach others. As you might imagine, my other hope is that you'll develop a more authentic and honest relationship with yourself and the people who matter the most in your life.

What I've learned more than anything else, and what my story has taught me, is that when you share what's deep inside, you're never truly alone.

This is the gift of story.

May my journey be a reminder to you that:

You don't have to have a big dramatic story to tell your story.

You don't need to be an award-winning writer to tell your story.

Having privilege doesn't prevent you from turning your story into something meaningful for the world.

Telling your story to the people you love the most can create the intimacy you long for.

FAQs about Telling Your Story

1. Why do I need to tell my story?

You don't. You get to decide. If you want to be able to build your relationship with any audience—whether it's an auditorium of people or conversation over lattes, or even yourself—your story is what will connect you to others. It's the glue.

2. Why am I so nervous about sharing my story?

Telling your story is an act of courage. We all hide. It's human nature. But why we hide and why we are afraid is unique to each one of us based on a set of circumstances, beliefs, and experiences from growing up. It's natural to be nervous about sharing your story. If you're nervous, I'd take that as a sign that you're about to grow.

3. If I start talking about my past, will I start sounding like a victim?

Telling your story isn't about blaming people or parts of your past. It's a forward-moving, forward-thinking activity that allows you to reflect on your past and make meaning from it. Story work helps you notice and express something important about yourself and how you see your world. It's about connecting the dots. Telling your story is a path to gaining insight about who you are.

4. How will I figure out what to include and what to take out?

Pain and struggle don't need to be exposed for exposure-sake. Sometimes TMI is exactly that: too much information. The stories you share have to do with the message you want to give. The stories you share need to be relevant and add to the momentum. You don't need to share everything, but you do need to let us in.

5. Why is telling your story so powerful?

Our stories are containers of our deepest emotions. Underneath those feelings are thoughts about ourselves. Telling our stories unleash those hidden scripts and beliefs. The healing comes from both the process and the outcome. That's the power of story. If you dig deep and learn about yourself, your story and the messages, people and experiences don't hold the same power over you.

A Framework for Telling Your Story

Every story has a beginning, middle and end. What I see in my work is that it can be important and profound to look at the **challenges** you've faced, the **choices** you've made and the **change** that comes as a result from the path you've taken. I call this **The Three C's** and organized this book according to these three parts of a story.

Challenge. This is the core struggle that you've faced in your life that keeps showing up in different circumstances again and again.

Choice. For most of us this is not one turning point, it is a series of choices that make up your life's journey.

Change. Most of us are scared of this word because we don't want to believe that we've changed. And yet, we have to own the way our life has moved in a different direction based on the choices that we've made.

No matter how you are planning to tell your story, I invite you to consider a beginning, middle, end that is informed by this simple yet powerful framework.

******

You can learn more about how to tell your story in my guide
Embrace Your Story Guide.
www.katherinekennedysf.com/embrace-your-story-guide

******

Visit my website for more inspiration and resources:
www.katherinekennedysf.com

GRATITUDE

I used to think the power in telling your story came from bringing what's inside into the light. Through writing this book and experiencing the process of telling my story, I now see another dimension…the TRUE power comes from finding and seeing the whole arc of the story…because when we find and see our story, we find and see the hero we possess inside.

And yet, all this *"hero-making"* isn't possible without the champions that are an integral part of my life! I can't begin to tell you how much support I needed not just to write this story but to put it into book form.

A huge thank you to ALL my champions:

Cara Jones, who helped me tap into my deepest wisdom and held my hand *[and heart]* throughout this entire process of excavating, revealing and writing my story. While we both believe in the power that comes from telling your story, I needed to be reminded of this constantly. Cara, you are a badass and all-around treasure. You have helped me *become.*

Kate Bonnycastle, who kept me laughing and believed in my writing and ability.

Jessica Sala-Bonin, I literally wouldn't have been able to execute this without you.

Cara Alter, Jeb Berkeley, Njeri Ndonga, KishaLynn Elliot, Jenni Calihan, and Lee Glickstein, who offered loving encouragement and wise counsel.

Allison, who was one of the first readers and helped me believe that this was a story worth sharing. And of course Susan, Jessica, Raleigh, Beth, Shafia, Erin, Courtney, Carolyn, Colby, Emily, Nina, Roslyn and Carrie, who also read a draft somewhere along this journey. I appreciate every ounce of encouragement, love and feedback that you gave me. I'm truly grateful to every single one of my friends and colleagues who have supported me on runs, hikes, drinks, dinner and conversations about this little book. Aren't we all happy to see it completed?!?

Linda, you gave me the tools to connect more deeply with the question *What's it like to be in your shoes?* that set me on a course for a more examined life and fulfilling work. I'm so grateful.

For my rocks Molly, Anne and Marty. It's a gift to have siblings that I've not only grown up with but whose love, support and deep friendship continues to inspire and sustain me.

Mom, you've given me the gift of your unconditional love, too. I feel you cheering me on, always. You and Dad showed us the way.

To my husband Duncan who is strong enough and generous enough to know that I needed to share this story, my truth. You help me on a daily basis to *be better than I used to be*. I love the life we are 'taking on' together. Thank you, thank you, *thank you* for loving me.

And to my kids. Charlie, Joey and Kate. You are the reason. I hope you know that you can, and always will, share what's inside.

Made in the USA
Monee, IL
01 October 2023

fbf17eec-d66b-4a47-bd6b-a57726925caaR01